Delirium

THE MISTAKEN CONFUSION

DEBRA CASON-MCNEELEY

PESI HEALTHCARE, LLC
PO Box 1000
200 Spring Street
Eau Claire, Wisconsin 54702

Printed in the United States of America

ISBN: 0-9722147-9-8

PESI HealthCare strives to obtain knowledgeable authors and faculty for its publications and seminars. The clinical recommendations contained herein are the result of extensive author research and review. Obviously, any recommendations for patient care must be held up against individual circumstances at hand. To the best of our knowledge any recommendations included by the author or faculty reflect currently accepted practice. However, these recommendations cannot be considered universal and complete. The authors and publisher repudiate any responsibility for unfavorable effects that result from information, recommendations, undetected omissions or errors. Professionals using this publication should research other original sources of authority as well.

For information on this and other PESI HealthCare manuals and audiocassettes, please call

800-843-7763

This work is dedicated to the love of my life, Stephen

ABOUT THE AUTHOR

Debra Cason-McNeeley, MSN, RNCS, began her nursing career 32 years ago and spent the initial 20 years in critical care before entering the mental health field. She completed her BSN at Grandview College, Des Moines, Iowa and received her MSN from the University of Northern Colorado, Greeley, Colorado. Debra has operated a private practice in massage therapy and geriatric assessment and counseling. She has taught and lectured nationally on topics related to the elderly, including end-of-life issues. Debra is currently certified as a Clinical Nurse Specialist in Adult Mental Health and Psychiatric Nursing through the American Nurses Credentialing Center. She is an adjunct professor in the BSN program at Mercy College of Health Sciences, and works part-time on an Inpatient Behavioral Health Unit.

TABLE OF CONTENTS

FOREWORD

It is 3 am in the small community hospital's emergency room. "Liz," an 18 year-old girl, has just arrived presenting with psychomotor agitation requiring restraints, and loud, pressured and disorganized speech. The ER staff attempts to engage her for clinical evaluation. She is patently uncooperative, responding more to her own internal stimuli than the focused questions of the clinicians. Perhaps it is not surprising that the busy ER physician decides it is time for a psychiatric consultation.

The young psychiatric resident examines the girl rapidly. A brief interview with her parents reveals that her behavioral symptoms have appeared over the last two weeks and have dramatically escalated in the last twenty-four hours. Given the clear psychosis evident, her demographic profile, and negative UDS, he concludes that she is experiencing her first psychotic break. He orders Haldol 5mg IM with Cogentin and writes up her mental health hold. Surely in the psychiatric ward her condition will be appropriately addressed and respond favorably.

Yet in the following thirty-six hours she becomes at times increasingly agitated, catatonically immobile at others, and her hallucinations are more prominent. The staff administered higher doses of her potent anti-psychotic medication, but somehow things still keep getting worse.

After two days this somewhat bemusing case takes a drastic and morbid turn. The adolescent goes into status epilepticus, her seizure terminated only after five long minutes. She is immediately sent back to the ER where she was initially categorized as a prototypical "psych patient." Now it is all too evident that her presenting symptoms, felt at first to be representative of a psychiatric condition, are in fact part of a systemic medical crisis: delirium.

Delirium is a syndrome made of behavioral symptoms that without careful practice are easily misinterpreted as etiologically psychiatric. By definition, it is not. Indeed, delirium pertains to disrupted central nervous system function brought about by dire medical and neurologic pathology. It occurs across the range of demographic groups. Particularly susceptible are those with the neuro-degenerative changes of certain age-related conditions. Sadly, clinicians everywhere from primary care, ER and med-surg to nursing home settings all too often miss the clues.

Why is such misdiagnosis so frequent? Largely, clinical naïveté and the diagnostic ambiguity often inherent in these cases. With virtually any behavioral syndrome, the formulation of a differential diagnosis that includes delirium should be an essential element of the clinician's professional competence.

As for "Liz," an MRI and lumbar puncture aided in the diagnosis of Herpes Encephalitis. The status epilepticus, brought about by the collusion of seizure threshold lowering infection and anti-psychotic medication, had left her vegetative.

The clinicians now understood. The misdiagnosis not only had denied her proper and rapid treatment, but also prompted iatrogenic catastrophe. The clues had been there all along, only the professional awareness was partially lacking. Thoughtful examination would have highlighted prominent short-term memory and attentional deficits uncommon for pure psychiatric states. In-depth interview with the parents would have revealed a recent history of intermittent bouts of anterograde amnesia.

Liz's story is true, and cases such as hers are all too prevalent. Thankfully, Debra Cason presents us with a concise yet comprehensive summation of delirium. I applaud her for providing a ready reference for such a dangerously under-emphasized syndrome with common presentation and potentially morbid consequences. Using the practices gleaned herein, we can all begin to help hone our diagnostic acumen in a truly vital area of medical care.

Daniel Fisher, MD
Chief of Staff
Director of Geriatric Services
Centennial Peaks Hospital
Louisville, Colorado

PREFACE

Recently there was a story on the local news. The story told of an 80-year-old woman who had hired a couple to live with her to assist her in her daily cares. During the eight months that ensued the woman grew seriously ill. She became confused, her memory was impaired and she could no longer manage her activities of daily living. Her family took her to the emergency room a total of thirteen times in this eight-month period. Every time they encountered the health care system, the family was told that the mental changes were due to her dementia. She had no previous diagnosis of dementia. She was never admitted to the hospital for a work-up, nor was any formal mental status testing performed. She was returned home, experienced functional decline and her family took her back to the hospital once again. Her family was keenly aware that something was wrong with their mother.

As it turns out, the care providers, hired to care for this woman, were administering her daily doses of benzodiazepines, antidepressants and sleeping medications. These medications had not been prescribed for her. Thank goodness the caregivers were caught and are awaiting prosecution.

While listening to this to this story I was struck by the fact that her family was aware that something was acutely wrong with their mother.

They took her to the hospital thirteen times in an eight-month period. Each time they were told that their mother was just old and failing due to dementia.

There are many story lines represented in this case but the one that speaks the loudest is the medical personnel's failure to recognize this acute condition of delirium. The changes evidenced by this woman were sudden and her family was the only one who recognized the sudden changes in their mother's abilities. Dementia is characterized by slow, progressive changes. Delirium is characterized by sudden and rapidly fluctuating changes in behavior and mentation. What saddens me the most is the fact that had it not been for the perseverance of this woman's family, she would had needlessly died, primarily from lack of knowledge by the physicians and nurses of the clinical presentation of delirium.

Delirium is often the underlying cause of altered behavior in the medically ill individual. It is rarely diagnosed and therefore not adequately treated. Delirium is a condition that overlaps medicine and psychiatry but is not owned by either discipline.

Individuals who demonstrate acute confusion are often dealing with a physical or mental illness known as delirium. If delirium is recognized and treated early, the course is temporary and reversible. The disorders that trigger delirium are diverse and plentiful. These triggers include deprivation of oxygen to the brain, diseases of other body systems, poisons, electrolyte imbalances, acute infections, and medications. If an individual has a pre-morbid brain condition, the likelihood of developing delirium increases significantly. Certain sectors of individuals are at a higher risk for the development of delirium than others, specifically the elderly.

The elderly are at the greatest risk for the development of delirium. Delirium also affects one in ten of patients who are hospitalized, whether for medical or psychiatric illnesses. Although these numbers reflect a high number of hospitalized patients, the diagnosis is often absent from the medical record. Due to the clinical presentation of confusion with increased anxiety and agitation, the individual is usually medicated to address the behavior not the underlying cause. These interventions often complicate the diagnosis and course of recovery.

It is imperative for all health care providers, regardless of their area of practice to educate them selves to the clinical presentation of delirium to facilitate early recognition and appropriate treatment. The intent of this book is to facilitate this learning process.

CHAPTER 1

History

The earliest Greek and Roman writers described conditions where febrile and toxic illnesses caused changes in perception, cognition, behavior and mood (Rabinowitz, 2002). Two terms were utilized to describe these changes. *Phrenitis* is the term for an agitated condition and *lethargus* described the condition represented by inactivity and somulence. The literature states that there are at least fifty-two names and/or phrases utilized that describe delirium. This is part of the difficulty in recognizing its presentation. Delirium is a serious medical condition. When it is merely identified as confusion with a possible modifier such as acute, the impetus for treating such status change as emergent is lost (Rockwood & Lindesay, 2002). This vast amount of descriptions also makes it difficult to conduct reliable research. In order to conduct valid and reliable research, variables must be accounted for. When delirium is not identified by its medical name, even if the clinical presentation meets the criteria, the ability to conduct respectable research is lost.

Historically, patients who are over 65 years of age represent one-third of hospital admission and 40% of physician office visits. With aging comes the decreased ability to maintain the delicate balance of equilibrium required for the body to function at its optimum. When this homeostatic balance is disrupted cognitive changes are commonly observed. This ability to maintain homeostasis is essential for the elderly individual to remain independent in the community. Independence allows the person to continue playing a contributing role in the community's development and progression. Independence enhances quality of life and contributes to a sense of integrity that is necessary during this stage of life.

CHAPTER 2

Definition

The DSM-IV TR defines delirium according to the following criteria:

A. Disturbance of consciousness (i.e., reduced clarity of awareness of the environment) with reduced ability to focus, sustain, or shift attention.

B. A change in cognition (such as memory deficit, disorientation, language disturbance) or the development of a perceptual disturbance that is not better accounted for by a preexisting, established, or evolving dementia.

C. The disturbance develops over a short period of time (actually hours to days) and tends to fluctuate during the course of the day.

D. There is evidence by history, physical examination, or laboratory findings that is caused by:

   1. A general medical condition
   2. Substance intoxication
   3. Substance withdrawal
   4. Multiple etiologies
   5. Not otherwise specified

CHAPTER 3

Clinical

Features

Delirium signifies a medical emergency. It is an acute, fluctuating change in mental status, with inattention and altered states of consciousness. It occurs suddenly, with noticeably significant decline from the individual's previous level of functioning. This sudden change in the level of functioning is not related to a preexisting condition or a developing dementia. Although the symptoms are wide ranging and non-specific, the fluctuating nature is a classic indicator of delirium. Cognitive changes, behavioral changes and depression are not part of the normal aging process. They are however, common. Distinguishing the underlying cause of these changes is the immediate goal.

When describing the cognitive or behavioral status of a person, the word "confused" is often used. Utilizing the term confusion, or documenting that a person is confused does not have the clinical pertinence as does stating that a person exhibits symptoms of delirium. Simply replacing the word confusion with the term delirium may prompt immediate interventions aimed at identifying the underlying cause of the change in the behavior that is displayed.

Symptoms of delirium typically become worse at night and this further clouds the clinical picture. Nurses report an increase in symptoms during the night and physicians see an entirely different individual during their daytime rounds. Accurate description of objective and subjective information provides the physician with the clinical picture necessary to identify delirium. When documentation includes the writer's bias or frustration, information is skewed, tainting the clinical picture.

Three subtypes of delirium have bee identified in the literature. These classifications are based on the level of activity observed. There is no established etiologic difference between the three subtypes. Hyperactive delirium occurs in about twenty-five percent (25%) of cases and exhibits as an increase in psychomotor activity and agitation. It is often misdiagnosed as anxiety or individual behaviors become troublesome and the patient is medicated to effect sedation. Individuals who display quiet behavior or a change from more active, alert involvement in their environment, to a more subdued and uninvolved interaction, typically do not receive the notice that people who display outwardly loud and challenging behavior do. If this hypoactive state is noticed, it is often misdiagnosed as depression. Treatment involves initiation of medication to treat the depression. This addition of medication contributes to exacerbating and complicating the delirium. Hypoactive delirium also represents twenty-five percent (25%) of cases and is evidenced by a decrease in psychomotor activity. Hypoactive delirium is misdiagnosed as depression or may be undetected. Hypoactive delirium carries with it a worse prognosis due to the changes displayed. These changes represent a quiet decline in the individual that puts them at risk for increased severity of illness, longer hospital stays, persistent delirium and higher death rates. Mixed delirium is a combination of hypoactive and hyperactive psychomotor activity and represents thirty-five percent (35%) of cases. About fifteen percent (15%) of individuals demonstrate normal psychomotor activity.

It is important to note that while mood disorders in the elderly are not uncommon, psychosis is. The person who is demented is not psychotic, particularly the individual with Alzheimer's disease. Due to the damage in the brain, people exhibit misidentifications and misrepresentations. These altered expressive and receptive mechanisms are not due to psychosis but to the neuronal death that accompanies Alzheimer's disease. Symptoms of psychosis seen in the elderly should immediately prompt suspicion of delirium.

Individuals who are experiencing delirium demonstrate a reduced level of lucidity but they do not reach the level of stupor or coma. Initially the person may appear disoriented which will progress to confusion. Their environment will appear unfamiliar. In addition, individuals will be unable to focus, sustain or shift their attention. Being easily distracted is often observed.

Disturbances in perception are common. These include illusions (misperceptions) and hallucinations (false perceptions or misidentifications). Typically hallucinations are of the visual variety but auditory hallucinations and other sensory modalities have been reported.

Other areas of cognitive function are also affected. These can include memory and visuoconstructional impairment, disorientation, or language disturbance. Recent memory is the most commonly influenced. Disorientation relates to time and/or place. Individuals believe they are in their home rather that the hospital or nursing home, or that it is day instead of night. Other people may not be recognized but disorientation to self is rare. Performing an assessment is challenging due to the persons inability to remain focused. However, regardless of how confused the individual might be, attempts at assessing must be made. Information obtained from the confused person is just as valuable as the information received from a more reliable source. Areas of impairment demonstrated by the confused person speak to the areas of the body affected by the condition of delirium and guide the practitioner towards suspected causes and treatment.

Delirium and dementia are defined in the DSM-IV TR but are also defined as medical conditions. Family members bring their loved ones to the medical clinic, psychiatric clinic or emergency room because of changes observed in the behavior of their loved ones. Chief complaints are often vague, i.e., he/she is just not their selves, or "one minute they are fine and the next they are wild."

In a study conducted by Fick and Foreman (2000), it was found that family members recognized abrupt changes in their loved ones.

However, Fick and Foreman also describe how physicians did not communicate with family members about these changes. Their study goes on to say that eighty-eight percent of people who demonstrate delirium superimposed on dementia were not recognized by health care providers.

Nurses and physicians specifically identified lack of knowledge as the reason for their lack of recognition of delirium. Observes in the study found that mental status was not assessed using formal instruments. If formal instruments are not used to identify changes from the person's baseline, delirium is unrecognized and the individual's condition continues in a downward spiral.

Following is a list of symptoms that would suggest delirium:

- Develops over short period of time, usually hours to days
- Fluctuates over the course of the day
- Direct result of general medical condition, substance intoxication or withdrawal, use of a medication, toxin exposure or combination of these
- Reduced awareness of environment
- Impaired ability to focus, sustain or shift attention
- Easily distracted
- Change in cognition (memory impairment, disorientation or language disturbance)
- Perceptual disturbance (misrepresentations, delusions or hallucinations)
- Speech and language disturbances (dysarthia, dysnomia, dysgraphia or aphasia)
- Disturbed sleep-wake cycle
- Disturbed psychomotor behavior
- Emotional disturbances

All behavior has meaning. It is a behavioral approach to fulfill an unmet need. All behavior is goal-directed. When people are born into this world, they lack verbal language skills. Humans make their needs known through their behavior. Parents quickly learn to recognize the subtleties of each cry, movement, squirm and smile. As children begin to grow, they relate their needs with increased non-verbal behavior. Temper tantrums are not uncommon. What is the physical, emotional or psychological need being expressed? Once again the parent who attends their child readily recognizes if the child is wet, tired, thirsty, sad, etc. This attention to detail of non-verbal communication is required of the care provider who cares for the client with cognitive impairment.

All behaviors, whether described as disturbing or delightful, should be understood to be a manner of communication. Disruptive behaviors may be an adaptive endeavor to preserve autonomy or may indicate the existence of other problems. Every behavior demonstrated by a person who is cognitively impaired has meaning. The responsibility of health care providers is to decipher the meaning and make every attempt to meet the expressed need. Using all five senses is crucial to interpreting what is being said through behavior.

Burgener & Dickerson-Putman (1999) found a significant relationship between negative feelings of staff toward the cognitively impaired client and the productive behaviors of the client. Healthcare providers who did not report episodes of aggressive behavior failed to do so because they felt the behavior was a result of a personal failure. If a change in behavior is not reported, delirium cannot be identified. The need to instantly end behaviors often overshadows the completion of a thorough assessment. Without an accurate assessment, treatment usually involves the administration of a chemical or physical restraint.

CHAPTER 4

Pathophysiology

Delirium is a generalized disorder of cerebral metabolism. While the neuropathophysiology of delirium is not definitive, a state of cholinergic decrease and dopamine increase is the predominant theory (Trzepacz & van der Mast, 2002). Delirium is also associated with electroencephalogram (EEG) slowing that is in line with wide spread cortical dysfunction. These abnormalities possibly provoke areas in the subcortical areas, specifically the brainstem and thalamus. Serotin also appears to be involved, both when levels are in excess or in deficient quantities. Levels of phenylalanine and tryptophan may also be abnormal. This abnormality is important to note due to the role of phenylalanine and tryptophan's in neurotransmitter synthesis. Levels of leukotrienes and interferons may also be elevated. Other hypotheses include a widespread reduction of oxidative metabolism, multiple neurotransmitter abnormalities, and increased levels of cerebral cytokines.

Certain medical conditions affect the ascending reticular activating system. Associated symptoms include attention, concentration and sleep-wake cycle deficits. The severity of delirium is influenced by the patient's pre-morbid medical condition.

Illness, surgery and trauma invoke the body's stress response. Originally designed as an adaptive response, prolonged exposure to these stressors triggers chemical reactions in the body. Activation of the sympathetic nervous system is the body's first response to stress. Cortisol levels rise and the immune response is activated. With prolonged stress cortisol levels remain elevated and the immune response is suppressed. This impacts the body's ability to heal. The biochemical changes associated with prolonged exposure to stress are also believed to cause delirium.

CHAPTER 5

Prevalence

All hospitalized patients are at risk for developing delirium. The statistics for medically ill individuals range from 10–30% and the hospitalized elderly have an incidence of 10–40%. Individuals who are inpatient for treatment of cancer experience a 25% chance of becoming delirious; individuals with AIDS exhibit delirium at a rate 0f 30–40%. Individuals undergoing surgery have a significant risk (51%) of becoming delirious and 80% of patients who are experiencing a terminal illness develop delirium. Sixty (60%) of individuals, age 70 and older, who reside in a long-term facility, are delirious. It has been estimated that misdiagnosis may occur in up to 80% of cases

Certain factors predispose an individual to the development of delirium. These include:

- Depression
- Drug use or dependence
- Infection
- Older age
- Poor premorbid functional status
- Preexisting cognitive impairment
- Recent surgery

- Severe chronic illness
- Trauma
- Visual impairment

Prevention

Potential Interventions for the Prevention of Delirium

Risk Factor	Intervention
Cognitive Impairment	• Routine mental status assessment • Education re: delirium for all staff • Orientation measures • Cognitive stimulating activities
Dehydration/Electrolyte Disturbance	• Early recognition • Intake and output recordings • Daily skin assessment • Access to fluids/assistance with fluid intake
Sensory Deprivation/ Sleep Disturbances	• Non-pharmacological sleep interventions • Noise and light reduction • Frequent rest periods

Potential Interventions for the
Prevention of Delirium (Continued)

Risk Factor	Intervention
Pharmacy/Use of psychoactive drugs	• Pharmacy liaison • Start low, go slow • Staff education regarding side effects • Choose non-anticholinergic medications • Routine medication assessment and evaluation
Malnutrition/Vitamin Nutrition assessment	• Deficiencies Monitoring of weight and height • Swallowing assessment • Feeding assistance • Nutritional support • B_{12}, B_1 deficiency assessment • Supplement when appropriate
Alcohol abuse	• Screening for alcohol abuse • Benzodiazepines for withdrawal management • Thiamine supplement
Immobilization	• Reduction of restraint usage • Active and passive range of motion • PT OT evaluation
Visual/Hearing Impairment	• Visual and hearing evaluations • Provision of assistive devices • Adequate lighting
Community-acquired infections	• Infection control measures • Proper and frequent handwashing • Antibiotic protocols • Avoidance of indwelling catheters

Potential Interventions for the
Prevention of Delirium (Continued)

Risk Factor	Intervention
Inadequate recognition of Delirium	• Educate patient/family at risk • Educate staff • Routine cognitive assessment with standard tools
Inadequate hospital care/systems failure	• Educate all health care professionals • Development of clinical guidelines for prevention, assessment and treatment • Initiate quality indicators to monitor for delirium

CHAPTER 7

Diagnosis

Two factors must be considered for accurate diagnosis. The first is recognizing the presence of delirium and the second is establishing the underlying cause. Failure to recognize or misdiagnoses occurs in 80% of cases.

"The diagnosis is in the history
if we choose to listen.
Unfortunately most of us are deaf."

Sir William Osler, M.D.

CHAPTER 8

Risk Factors

Patient's factors

Individual:

- Age
- Pre-existing cognitive deficits
- Severe comorbidity
- Previous episode of delirium
- Personality before illness

Perioperative:

- Course of postoperative period
- Type of operation (hip replacement)
- Emergency operation
- Duration of operation

Specific condition:

- Burns; AIDS; fracture; metabolic disturbance; hypoxemia; organ insufficiency

Pharmacological factors

- Treatment with many drugs
- Dependence on drugs or alcohol
- Use of psychoactive drugs or alcohol
- Specific drugs that may cause problems
    - Benzodiazepines
    - Anticholinergic agents
    - Narcotics

Environmental factors

- Extremes in sensory experiences
- Deficits in hearing or vision
- Immobility or decreased activity
- Novel environment
- Stress

CHAPTER 9

Clinical
Course

E arly signs of delirium, called prodromal symptoms are generally
observed 1–3 days prior to symptoms of full-blown delirium.
These early indicators include: restlessness, anxiety, irritability, dis-
tractibility or sleep disturbances. If symptoms are not recognized or are
misdiagnosed, delirium will progress.

Resolution of symptoms depends on accurate diagnosis. Research
suggests the general course of delirium lasts from less than one week
to more than two months. If the cause is identified and addressed, delirium may resolve within 10–12 days, however it is not unusual for
symptoms to persist for 30 days and beyond. The elderly have demonstrated a prolonged course, frequently exceeding one month.

Most individuals recover fully, however, delirium can progress to
stupor, coma, seizures and death. The risk for progression is greatest if
delirium undiagnosed and untreated. The elderly have a low percentage
of recovering fully prior to discharge from a hospital. At discharge it is
estimated that the elderly have only a 4–40% chance of resolution of
symptoms. It is not uncommon for the elderly patient to experience persistent cognitive deficits following recovery from delirium.

Significant morbidity is also associated with delirium, especially in the elderly population. The risk of complications such as pneumonia, and decubitus ulcers are common. Postoperative recovery is extended with poor outcomes. Hospital stays are prolonged if complications occur. These complications significantly increase the financial burden for patients, hospitals, and physicians. In addition to increased medical costs, complications also place an unbalanced proportion of healthcare resources on a limited few.

Mortality rates also increase in individuals who experience delirium. The elderly in particular are at a 22–76% risk of dying during hospitalization and during the months that follow. It is suggested that patients who become delirious during their inpatient hospitalization die within 6 months and that death within 3 months of diagnosis is 14 times higher than average.

Differentiating Between Delirium, Dementia, and Depression

Clinical Feature	Delirium	Dementia	Depression
Onset	Acute/subacute; depends on the cause	Chronic, generally insidious	Coincides with life changes; often abrupt
Course	Short, fluctuating, worse at night, dark and upon awakening	Long, no diurnal effects, symptoms progressive yet stable over time	Diurnal effects; typically worse in morning; situational fluctuations
Duration	Hours to weeks	Months to years	Weeks, months, years
Alertness	Fluctuates	Generally normal	Normal
Orientation	Fluctuates; generally impaired	May be impaired	May be impaired

Differentiating Between Delirium, Dementia, and Depression (Continued)

Clinical Feature	Delirium	Dementia	Depression
Memory	Recent/immediate impaired; remote intact	Recent and remote impaired	Difficulty with abstraction; vague
Thinking	Disorganized, distorted, fragmented, slow or accelerated	Difficulty with abstraction; vague	Intact; often slowed
Perception	Distorted, illusions, delusions	Misperceptions often absent	Variable, hallucinations
Psychomotor behavior	Variable; hypo or hyper-kinetic or mixed	Variable	Normally or minimally hypokinetic
Attention	Impaired	Normal except in advanced dementia	May be disordered
Physical illness/ drug toxicity	One or both present	One or both present	Usually absent, debatable
Sleep/wake cycle	Disturbed; cycle reversed	Fragmented	Disturbed
Associated features	Variable affective changes; symptoms of autonomic arousal	Affect tends to be superficial, labile and inappropriate	Affect depressed; dysphoric mood; exaggerated and detailed complaints

CHAPTER 10

Causes

A ny number of agents or conditions can lead to delirium. The most common precursors include medications, medical conditions, and poisons. The decreased reserve capacity in the brain of the aging person makes them less adaptable to the stress of acute illness, medications and changes in their environment.

Medications, while prescribed to improve symptoms and medical conditions, pose certain risks. All medications have the potential for causing side effects. In addition, when combining medications in an effort to treat various conditions, the risk multiplies. Each time a medication is added to an existing regime, the potential for drug-to-drug interaction exists. Each adjustment of dosage must also be identified as a potential for complications.

Medications that cause delirium

- Anticholinergics, antihistamines, antiparkinsonian agents, muscle relaxants, phenothiazines, tricyclic antidepressants
- Sedatives, including barbiturates, benzodiazepines, and ethanol
- Antidepressant drugs
- Corticosteroids
- Anticonvulsant drugs
- Analgesics such as narcotics, non-steroidal anti-inflammatory drugs (NSAIDs), opiods

- Cardiovascular agents such as antiarrhythmic agents, antihypertensive agents, Digoxin
- Lithium
- Cimetidine
- Antibiotics such as aminoglycosides, cephalosporins, penicillins
- L-dopa
- Antiemetics
- Antiasthmatic agents
- Immunosuppressive agents

When considering prescribing medications or just reviewing the list of current medications the elderly individual is taking, certain factors must be taken into account. These include:

Changes in absorption and distribution due to aging

Slower absorption:

- oral and parenteral medications
- medications requiring acidic medium due to decreased acidity of the GI tract, e.g., NSAIDs
- suppositories due to decreased blood supply to the rectum and lower core body temperature

Slower distribution:

- due to reduction of active and passive transport system

Increased amount of pharmacologically active drug:

- due to fewer amounts of plasma proteins that are available for binding

Slower drug metabolism and longer duration of action:

- Resulting from decreased liver enzyme production caused by decreased circulation to the liver

Increased concentration:

- Resulting from decreased body mass and surface area

Decreased excretion:

- Due to decreased renal function

May have **normal serum creatinine** but **abnormal creatinine clearance**

Changes Affecting Drug Disposition in the Elderly

Pharmacokinetic Parameter	Physiological Change
Absorption time	↑ Gastric pH ↓ Gastric Emptying ↓ GI motility ↓ GI blood flow
Distribution	↓ Lean muscle
Mass	↓ Total body ↑ Total body fat
Water	↓ Serum albumin ↓ Cardiac output
Metabolism	↓ Liver mass ↓ Hepatic blood flow ↓ Enzyme activity
Excretion	↓ Renal blood flow ↓ Glomerular filtration rate ↓ Renal tubular function

Other Important Tips

1. For persons 65–80, staring dose should be reduced by $1/2$
2. For persons > 80, starting dose should be reduced by $2/5$
3. Absolutely any medication can cause mental status changes
4. People who take > 3–4 meds, including OTCs, are at a very high risk for drug/drug interaction. The more meds, the higher the risk.

5. Tricyclic antidepressants and benzodiazepines will likely cause confusion

6. Sedatives and analgesics are the nest group causing confusion

Psychoactive substances that cause delirium

- Ethanol
- Marijuana
- LSD
- Amphetamines
- Cocaine
- Opiates
- PCP
- Inhalants

Poisons that cause delirium

- Solvents such as gasoline, kerosene, turpentine, benzene, and alcohols
- Carbon monoxide
- Refrigerants, Freon
- Heavy metals such as lead, mercury, and arsenic
- Insecticides such as Parathion and Sevin
- Mushrooms such as Amanita species
- Plants such as jimsonweed and morning glory
- Animal venoms
- Carbon dioxide

Medical conditions that cause delirium

Systemic illness

- Substance intoxication or withdrawal
- Infection, especially urinary tract infection
- Neoplasm
- Severe trauma
- Sensory deprivation
- Temperature dysregulation
- Postoperative state

Metabolic Disorders

- Renal failure
- Hepatic Failure
- Anemia
- Hypoxia
- Hypoglycemia/hyperglycemia
- Hypothyroid/hyperthyroid
- Thiamine deficiency
- Endocrinopathy
- Fluid or electrolyte imbalance
- Acid base imbalance

Cardiopulmonary disorders

- Myocardial failure
- Congestive heart failure
- Cardiac arrhythmia
- Shock
- Respiratory failure
- Chronic obstructive pulmonary disease
- Pneumonia
- Pulmonary embolus
- Hypoxia

Central Nervous System Disorders

- Head trauma
- Seizures
- Postdictal state
- Vascular disease
- Degenerative disease

Intracranial processes

- Dementia
- Hematoma
- Malignancy
- Meningitis
- Stroke

Other

- Stroke
- Fecal impaction
- Vitamin deficiencies
- Fever
- Fluid and electrolyte imbalances
- Post surgical complication

Examples of conditions that lead to delirium and are easily reversed are listed below.

- Hypoglycemia
- Hypoxia or anoxia
- Hyperthermia
- Alcohol or sedative withdrawal
- Wernicke's encephalopathy
- Anticholinergic delirium
- Severe hypertension

CHAPTER 11

Assessment

The goal of treating delirium is identification of the underlying cause. To facilitate this, a thorough assessment must be completed. While the patient may not be the most reliable resource for gathering information, it is important to attempt an interview and observe behaviors. Other sources must also be utilized for gathering information; these include family, care providers, primary care practitioners and past medical records. When requesting information regarding medications, consulting the pharmacy where the individual purchases their medications would provide the most accurate information. Below is a list of essential assessment tools required for accurate diagnosis.

- Complete medical history
- Medical conditions (when diagnosed, how treated, compliance with treatment)
- Medications (name, dosage, frequency, reason, when started, dosage change, compliance)
- Past surgeries (when, complications, recovery course)
- Physical and neurological examination
- Vital signs and anesthesia if postoperative
- Review of medical record (current and past)

- Mental status examination
- Interview
- Cognitive testing (MMSE, clock drawing, Hodkinson mental test etc.)
- Basic laboratory test
- CBC
- Comprehensive chemistry (electrolytes, glucose, calcium, albumin, blood urea nitrogen, alkaline phosphate, creatinine, SGOT, SGTP, bilirubin, magnesium, PO4
- Electrocardiogram
- Chest x-ray
- Arterial blood gases or pulse oximetry
- Urinalysis with culture and sensitivity
- Additional laboratory tests (ordered as indicated by clinical condition &/or history)
- VDRL, heavy metal screen, B_{12} & folate levels, lupes erythematosus prep, antinuclear antibody, urinary porphyrins, ammonia, human immunodeficiency virus, Blood cultures
- Measurement of serum levels of medications (e.g. digoxin, theophyllin, phenobarbital, cyclosporin
- Lumbar puncture
- CT or MRI
- EEG

While waiting for more definitive information on possible causes, it is important to monitor the patient closely. These indicators should include vital signs, oxygenation, fluid intake and output. In addition, a careful assessment of the patient's medications should be completed and all non-essential medications should be discontinued, and doses of essential medications should be changed to the lowest possible dose.

In addition to the above testing, information regarding symptoms should be obtained. Categories to be covered when questioning the patient and/or their family include:

Language symptoms

- Noticeable changes in Language
- Cannot think of the right word
- Forget the name of objects
- Trouble comprehending

Memory Symptoms

- Memory problem
- When did the problem begin
- Onset—sudden or gradual
- Is memory better, the same or worse

Personality Changes

- Noticeable change in personality
- Change in social activities
- More argumentative or irritable
- Passive or apathetic
- More depressed

Family Interview/Activities of Daily Living

- Trouble taking medications
- Trouble managing finances
- Neglect in appearance or hygiene
- Trouble in unfamiliar surroundings

Assessment of Delirium

Clinical Feature	How to Assess
Level of Consciousness	Observe for changes in level of consciousness. Alert, hyperalert (easily startled), lethargic, stupor, coma

Assessment of Delirium (Continued)

Clinical Feature	How to Assess
Behavior	Observe behavior: calm, withdrawn, fidgety, hyperactive, psychomotor agitation, picking at bed clothing, pulling at tubing, wandering, trying to get out of bed, yelling crying, etc.
Orientation	Ask the patient: • What is your full name? • Can you identify members of your immediate family? • What is today's date, month, day of week, year season? • What is the name of this place, city state? • Why were you admitted?
Attention	Ask the patient to complete a two part command: "roll up your sleeve and extend you arm for a BP check" Ask them to spell a word backward (note latent responses, difficulty following directions, decreased attention)
Memory	Ask the patient to demonstrate the use of the call bell system, in five minutes ask them to perform. Ask to repeat 5 objects and repeat in 5 minutes.
Perceptual disturbances	Ask the patient if he is hearing or seeing things in his room when no one is around. Ask if he feels frightened or believes he's in danger. Observe for responses to unseen stimuli
Thought processes	Engage in conversation. Can they focus on the conversation? Does their speech make sense?
Affect	Inquire about mood. Observe affect. Is it consistent or does it vary? Describe affect.
Physical	Observe for motor abnormalities. Observe for gait disturbances.

CHAPTER 12

Management

Flacker and Marcantonio (1998) offer a five-step approach to managing delirium. The first step involves defining delirium using the DSM-IV TR or the Confusion Assessment Method (CAM). The next step involves identifying patients who are inherently at risk for its development. The third step involves improved recognition. The fourth step is to adequately assess the patient to identify contributing factors. Finally, management is crucial.

As stated earlier, a vast number of terms are used to describe delirium. Avoiding all other descriptions would assist the practitioner in ready recognition and eliminate inaccurate diagnosis. Delirium is defined in the DSM-IV TR. Unfortunately the DSM-IV TR is utilized primarily by psychiatric practitioners. If would behoove medical practitioners to familiarize themselves with its contents as it provides clear definitions and criteria for many conditions that are not limited to psychiatric practice. Once delirium is defined, it is important to identify populations who are at risk for its development.

In order to prevent delirium from developing, or limiting its course once it has developed, it is important to identify populations who are at risk for its occurrence. Delirium can affect individuals of all ages, although certain groups are inherently at risk. Persons at the extreme ends of age are of particular risk. The very young and the very old do not have the physiological ability to rapidly return the body to its cherished equilibratory state. Individuals who qualify as extremely vulnerable are also at risk. Examples include people with a diagnosis of a serious medical condition like an acute autoimmune disorder, diabetes, or a neuromuscular disorder, to name a few. Even the most minor insult can produce delirium in this group. Possessing a clear sense of deliriums definition and an awareness of those at risk is not sufficient to manage delirium. A person must also possess the clinical skills necessary to suspect and recognize its presentation.

Flacker and Marcantonio (1988) address a study involving 250 elderly emergency room patients. The results of the study found that 10% of these individuals met the criteria for delirium yet only 13% had a note that indicated recognition of a mental status change. No further testing was conducted to ascertain the cause of the behavioral change. In addition, 29% of the participants were subsequently discharged back to their home and faced future complications. Failure to recognize delirium not only occurs in the emergency room, medical and surgical patients fare no better. A study involving 111 patients with a femoral neck fracture revealed that 61.3% of patients were found to have postoperative delirium. Of these cases, 38.8% of documentation by nursing staff addressed the mental status changes and only 8.1% had any documentation by a physician recognizing such changes. These studies provide invaluable information about the blatant lack of recognition of delirium that occurs in all arena of practice. When delirium is not recognized, it cannot be adequately managed, and yet, diagnosis is only the first step of management.

Although diagnosis is important, it is not the most significant piece of the puzzle. Identification of the causative factors outweighs the diagnosis in it's importance. This step involves careful assessment outlined previously. Regardless of the status of assessment, management must begin at the point of initial contact with the patient.

Management involves treating the primary cause of delirium, avoiding iatrogenic complications, remove any contributing factors, maintain patient safety and provide support for the patient and their family. This approach requires a cohesive, multi-disciplinary approach. Management of the client with delirium is extremely labor intensive but well worth the effort for avoiding complications. These complications are devastating for the client from a psychological, physical, emotional, spiritual and financial perspective.

Four main aspects for managing delirium have been identified. These include:

- Identifying and treating the underlying causes
- Providing environmental and supportive measures
- Prescribing medications aimed at managing symptoms and providing safety
- Regular clinical review and follow-up

Interventions to prevent and/or treat delirium*

Environmental Modifications	Unit-wide noise reduction
	Orienting objects
	Safe and familiar environment
	Using personal objects
	Diurnal variation of noise and light
	Orientation cues
	Strategies to familiarize environment
Psychological Support	Cognitive stimulation
	"Touch" contact with family
	Music and television for stimulation
	Conversational interactions with staff and peers
	Consultation with geriatric nurse liaison

---

* Source: Foreman, M, Wakefield, B, Culp, K, & Milisen, K. (2001). Delirium in elderly patients: An overview of the state of the science. Journal of Gerontological Nursing, April, 12–20.

Interventions to prevent and/or treat delirium (Continued)

Physiologic Stability	Early recognition of dehydration Encouragement of fluids Monitoring oxygenation Nutritional support Early recognition of urinary tract infection Monitoring of response to change in medication
Support of Sensory Function	Visual aids and adaptive devices Amplification devices, earwax removal, routine battery change Use of appropriate sensory aids
Physical Activity	Minimize sensory deprivation Ambulation and active/passive range of motion Physical therapy, Occupational therapy

---

Interventions for the treatment of Delirium

Providing Support and Orientation

- Communicate clearly and concisely
- Give repeated verbal reminders of the time, day, location, and identity of key individuals, such as members of family and key treatment team members
- Provide clear signposts to patient's location including a clock, calendar, chart with the day's schedule
- Have familiar objects from the patient's home in the room
- Use a TV or radio for relaxation and to help the patient maintain contact with the outside world
- Involve family and caregivers to encourage feelings of security and orientation
- Ensure consistency of staff

Providing an Unambiguous Environment

- Ensure adequate warmth and nutrition
- Simplify care areas by removing unnecessary objects
- Allow adequate space between beds
- Consider using single rooms to aid rest and avoid extremes of sensory experience
- Avoid using medical jargon in the patient's presence to decrease the risk of paranoia
- Ensure adequate lighting (a 40–60 watt light lessens the chance of misperceptions)
- Control sources of excess noise (< 45 decibels during the day and < 20 decibels at night)
- Keep room temperature between 21.1° C to 23.8° C

Maintaining Competence of the Individual

- Identify and correct sensory impairments
- Ensure patients have glasses (correct prescription), hearing aids (fresh batteries), & dentures
- Consider if an interpreter is necessary
- Encourage self-care and participation in treatment
- Arrange treatments to allow maximum periods of rest and uninterrupted sleep
- Maintain activity levels
- Ambulatory patients should walk three times per day
- Include a full range of motion for all joints three times per day

The use of physical restraints should be avoided

Ensure Safe environment

Basic changes can be incorporated for healthcare providers that will enable the practitioner to recognize and intervene in patients who exhibit delirium. These include:

a. Eliminate the word "confusion" from your vocabulary. Replace it with accurate objective documentation of observed behaviors.

b. Incorporate yearly competencies of geriatric health care, including signs and symptoms of delirium

c. Incorporated standard instruments for screening symptoms designed for the recognition of acute mental status changes.

DRUG TREATMENT FOR DELIRIUM

T he current age of pharmaceuticals is wondrous. Many diseases are now treatable if not curable. However, medications do not work on behavior unless there is an underlying physiological rationale for the behavior. Careful attention must be made before considering medication management of delirium. Medications are one of the most significant risk factors for the development of delirium and utilizing them for management can complicate the clinical picture. Psychotropic medications can skew the mental status assessment and increase the patient's risk for falling. Sedatives may subdue behavior but cloud cognitive abilities.

Neuroleptics improve numerous symptoms related to hyperactive and hypoactive delirium (Meagher, 2001). Their onset is rapid and improvement is evident within hours, however the underlying cause remains unchanged. If medications are chosen for use in treating delirium, neuroleptics are the drug of choice in all cases except with drug and alcohol withdrawal.

Haloperidol is the drug of choice due to it's limited anticholinergic effects, fewer active metabolites, less sedation and hypotensive effects and it can be administered by a variety of routes. Haloperidol usage does bring with it the increased risk of extrapyramidal side effects. Using Haloperidol intravenously appears to have less risk of inducing extrapyramidal side effects in the client with delirium. Dosage of antipsychotic medication depends on the route of administration, desired effect, patient age, risk of side effects and the therapeutic setting. For oral usage of Haloperidol, initial dosing of 1–10 mg per 24 hours has been shown to be effective (Meagher, 2001).

Olanzapine and respiridone have demonstrated success in treating symptoms of delirium. These medications have a smaller risk of producing extrapyramidal side effects and cause less sedation, however, they are only available in oral form. Limited studies of low dose use of trazadone and mianserin have shown to produce a rapid decrease in non-cognitive symptoms of delirium.

Benzodiazepines are the first line drug of choice for seizures and withdrawal from alcohol or sedatives. The therapeutic goal should be precise since increased side effects of sedation are dose dependent.. Lorazepam is a favorable choice due to it's rapid onset, short duration of action, low risk of accumulation and lack of active metabolites. It is readily bioavailable when given intramuscularly. Recommended upper dose limits are 2 mg every four (4) hours.

It is imperative to consider the rationale for consideration of medication usage. Are medications utilized for the benefit of the patient or for the benefit of staff? The behavior demonstrated by individuals with delirium can be troubling for staff, but not nearly as distressing as they are for the person. It is important to remember that medications that sedate cause more complications for the patient than they solve.

CHAPTER 13

Delirium with Acute Alcohol/Substance Intoxication/Withdrawal

A cute alcohol or other substance ingestion or withdrawal can cause sudden changes in mentation and physical functioning of the body. It is considered a serious medical/mental event with the potential for life-threatening consequences. In addition to ingestion, withdrawal from alcohol and/or other substances poses serious medical/cognitive complications that can lead to death. The incidence of complicated withdrawal (delirium tremens) is rare, 1 out of 10,000 people will be affected. Risks for developing delirium include acute binge intake of large quantities of alcohol and/or other substances or sudden abstinence following daily use of large quantities of alcohol and/or other substances, as well as those with a habitual use or alcoholism that has existed for more than 10 years.

When monitoring for symptoms of withdrawal, it is important to remember that total detoxification, or blood levels declining to zero are not the stimulus for complications. Instead, complications occur when changes in the blood concentration take place rapidly. The change in the blood concentration is the predictive factor for complications. Mortality rates have been reported as high as 15–20%. These numbers increase when a comprehensive history has not been obtained and care providers lack information that would indicate significant patient risk.

Symptoms of abrupt stoppage of significant alcohol intake include:

- Increase in pulse, blood pressure, respiratory rate and temperature
- Feeling jumpy or nervous
- Feeling shaky; visible tremors
- Anxiety
- Irritability, or easily excited
- Emotional volatility, rapid emotional changes
- Depression
- Fatigue
- Difficulty thinking clearly
- Palpitations (feeling heart beat in the chest of feelings of the heart fluttering)
- Headache, usually pulsating
- Sweating, especially the palms of the hands
- Nausea, vomiting
- Anorexia
- Insomnia, difficulty falling asleep
- Pale skin with flushing of the face

Mental status changes:

- Rapid mood changes
- Restlessness
- Increased activity, inability to sit still
- Decreased attention span
- Excitement
- Fear
- Confusion, disorientation
- Agitation, irritability

- Hallucinations, usually visual
- Sensory hyperactivity (sensitive to light, sounds, and touch
- Delirium
- Decreased mental status (stupor, somnolence, lethargy, deep sleep lasting for a day)
- Seizures: generalized tonic-clonic; initial 72 hours greatest risk, greater risk with previous withdrawal complications
- Fever, stomach pain, chest pain

To effectively manage acute alcohol intoxication/withdrawal is must be considered a medical emergency. Assessing the neuromuscular system for increased startle reflex, rapid rhythmic muscle tremor or other changes listed above indicates the possibility of this crisis. Dehydration, electrolyte imbalance, and malnutrition may also be evident. It is important to consider obtaining serum toxicology for the blood alcohol levels as well a comprehensive blood chemistry. The results may reveal decreased levels of magnesium and potassium. Arrhythmias may be evident on the electrocardiogram (EKG).

The goal of intervention is the saving of the patient's life, treating the presenting symptoms and preventing complications. It necessary to hospitalize the patient throughout the initial seventy-two hour period to adequately manage symptoms and monitor for life threatening complications. These include life support efforts, anticonvulsant medications, medications to treat cardiovascular complications, hydration, nutrition, and sedation to decrease tremors and agitation. Antipsychotic medications to treat hallucinations are not generally recommended. It is also important to address underlying medical issues such as liver impairment, blood clotting disorders, heart disorders and chronic brain impairments. Potential complications of acute intoxication/withdrawal also include injury from falls and potential injury to self and others resulting from the confused mental state.

Once the initial crisis has passed, the individual will continue to experience residual symptoms of fatigue, depression, anxiety and insomnia for up to one year. Medical conditions should be treated and followed closely as required by the condition. These conditions include:

alcoholic neuropathy, cardiac disorders, chronic brain disorders, liver disease and blood clotting disorders.

Following recovery from withdrawal, some conditions may exhibit themselves. These include apathy, insomnia, fatigue and emotional liability. It is not uncommon for the individual to experience these symptoms for one year or more. If mood disorders persist, a referral to a psychiatrist would be appropriate.

Prevention involves abstinence of using alcohol. Treatment for substance abuse is recommended

CHAPTER 14

Delirium in the Critical Care Unit

It is estimated that 15–40% of patients in critical care units are delirious. The elderly and males following cardiac surgery have the highest risk. This increased number of patients with delirium is due in part, to the increased number of elderly being hospitalized and the seriousness of illness that are currently being treated. In addition, patients are given potent psychoactive medications such as benzodiazepines and opiates in order to perform invasive procedures and perform life-saving measures. These medications can lead to changes in cognitive functioning. Truman & Wesley (2003) state that while 8 of 10 patients in the ICU display symptoms of delirium, it is unrecognized in 66–84% of patients. The incidence of delirium will undoubtedly increase as patient age rises, and as the number of chronic illnesses each person experiences intensify.

Nurses who work in intensive care units are familiar with the term "ICU psychosis." Many ICU staff consider it a normal response. It is considered a side effect of medical conditions, medications, anesthesia, and increased/decreased sensory stimulation. This cognitive impairment is expected, temporary and thought to have little consequence. Research is now telling us that this alteration in cognitive function is consistent with delirium and its presence lengthens hospital stays, prolongs neurological recovery, increases placement in care centers following discharge, and increases mortality rates. The assessment tool for identifying delirium, the CAM, has been modified for intensive care units.

An example of this happened to Mr. F.

Mr. F. was a 72 year old gentleman who was admitted to the hospital for coronary artery bypass surgery. There was no mention on his medical record that Mr. F had a twenty-year history of daily alcohol intake. It is unknown whether this information was requested or if the patient denied his use. Twenty-four hours following surgery Mr. F became acutely confused. He proceeded to pull out his intubation tube, chest tubes, arterial line, nasogastric tube, cardiac pacing wires and his foley catheter. Subsequently he developed a sternal infection that required a return to surgery for debriedment. Upon his return form this second surgery his status was extremely critical. It was after his second surgery that the staff learned of his chronic alcohol consumption. He was placed on a continuous alcohol drip via intravenous fluids. In addition to his alcohol drip he was kept paralyzed through the use of intravenous medication.

Mr. F. care required that two nursing staff dress in sterile surgical attire and perform sterile irrigation of his chest wound every four hours. This procedure was delicate and potentially life threatening. Mr. F. recovered after a lengthy stay in the surgical intensive care unit followed by another lengthy stay in the hospital on a intermediate floor. As he recovered from his sternal infection and his condition improved he was slowly weaned off the alcohol drip. He did not suffer any withdrawal complications during this period.

What is normally a seven-day recovery period following coronary artery bypass surgery turned into a two-month stay for Mr. F. In addition to his prolonged hospitalization, Mr. F. and his family faced a life-threatening complication that could have been avoided if the right questions had been asked during his pre-surgical history. Mr. F faced long-term placement following hospital discharge due to his compromised physical condition. He required extensive rehabilitation from physical therapy due to his weakened state. From a monetary perspective, his care cost four to five times what is would have if he had hot suffered such severe complications. The money spent for his extended had the potential of impacting the care another person might have required. Mr. F was in an intensive unit four times longer than most and it is unknown what impact this had on the patients who might have needed a bed in this unit. Increased health-care costs, utilization of resources, increased morbidity and potential mortality were the outcomes of this failure to recognize delirium and its cause in the case of Mr. F.

Interventions for patients in the ICU who experience delirium include modifications to alleviate sleep disruption, reduction of noise levels, communication with patients regardless of their consciousness level, reorientation, relaxed visiting regulations which allows for continuous support from loved ones, and ensuring adequate pain relief. On average, patients in ICU are disrupted every twenty minutes. Sleep is the body's mechanism for healing. If the body is deprived an opportunity to promote healing, healing requires longer periods of time and complications are provided an opportunistic environment.

Another area that can be modified is lighting. Having lights on during the day and kept as low as possible during the night allow the body to maintain its circadian rhythm. Staff working in ICU have adapted to the constant and varying noises that are continuously heard throughout the unit. Patients in ICU often misinterpret these sounds. It is recommended that equipment be moved as far away from patients as possible and that alarms be softened. Reorientation is a must every time a nurse encounters a patient. This constant reminder offers the patient information that relieves confusion and in turn, lessens anxiety. Frequent monitoring of pain, especially when the patient is unable to communicate their needs relieves stress and frustration. Pain relief also allows the patient an opportunity for quality sleep.

Note: Brenda Truman has offered a free training manual that includes CD videos and a kit to complete the CAM ICU. She can be reached at:

Brenda.Truman@vanderbilt.edu

Delirium in the Emergency Room

T he elderly arrive at the emergency room with multiple and more complex conditions than their younger counterparts. Assessment in the emergency room begins with a chief complaint and then a thorough history. Elderly people typically do not report one chief complaint but rather report several complaints related to existing chronic illnesses. It is important to also note that the complaints may appear vague in nature. The elderly comprise 20% of emergency room patients. This figure is significantly higher than the 14% they represent in the general population.

Sanders (2002) states that 26–40% of older persons arriving in the emergency room demonstrate cognitive impairment or delirium. He goes on to state that emergency room personnel recognize only 17–33% of individuals with delirium. Many patients are sent home without proper recognition of this serious condition. In addition to assessing physical complaints, it is imperative for emergency personnel to assess cognitive status of all elderly clients who are seen. This can be accomplished by the use of formal mental status assessment instruments and accurate, objective documentation of observations. Family members or staff from referring facilities can provide invaluable base-line level of functioning.

CHAPTER 16

Delirium in the Hospital

M rs. C, an 81-year-old female consented to elective hip replacement surgery. Prior to surgery she had been living alone at an adult apartment complex. She had been widowed for three years. Her children lived in various states and visited infrequently. She cooked her own meals and was independent with her daily living activities. She had given up driving but continued to enjoy working with the flowers in the garden of the apartment complex.

Following surgery Mrs. C demonstrated acute confusion with an inability to focus attention. She also experienced visual hallucinations where she said her dead husband in the room with her. Her primary care physician documented that she was confused and prior to her discharge he wrote in her progress notes: "remains confused and disoriented stemming from her dementia." The nursing notes reflected "inappropriate behavior and inappropriate answers to questions." No further description of her inappropriateness was found in the nursing documentation. There was no evidence of formal mental status testing by the physician or the nursing staff. Mrs. C. was discharged to a nursing home where she continued to decline and dies five months following her admission.

This case emphasizes the lack of recognition of delirium in the patient who is diagnosed with dementia. Any change in cognitive functioning is considered to stem from dementia rather than from a potentially acute condition. Once an individual is diagnosed with dementia conduction of formal testing of mental status ceases. The focus switches to the behavior demonstrated rather than a potential underlying cause of the behavior change. While a change in behavior is sometimes documented, no further testing is conducted to elicit its potential etiology

Hospitalized medically ill patients	10–30%
Hospitalized elderly patients	10–40%
Hospitalized cancer patients	25%
Hospitalized AIDS patients	30–40%
Terminally ill patients	80%

Delirium is the most frequent complication facing the hospitalized elderly patient (Inouye, 2002). The yearly number of elderly people who become delirium during hospitalization has reached 2.3 million. This represents 17.5 million inpatient days and costs $4 billion (1994 US dollars). Following discharge from the hospital, the cost continues to climb due to extended care placement, rehabilitation, home care services and pharmaceutical costs.

It has been suggested that 10–15% of elderly exhibit symptoms upon admission, and 5–40% develop symptoms during hospitalization. These numbers have a significant impact on the recovery rates of these individuals. Mortality rates increase to 25–33%. Increased morbidity, global functional decline and placement in long-term facilities have also been demonstrated. Other considerations include an increase in hospital costs incurred and secondary complications.

When delirium is not recognized and interventions are not initiated to alleviate the condition, complications ensue. This results in higher hospital costs, post-anesthesia complications, and increased morbidity and mortality. Hospital rates for hospitalized patients who are delirious are significant at 10–65%. Other complications result from lack of recognition regarding delirium. These include cardiac arrest, ventricular tachycardia, or fibrillation, myocardial infarction, pulmonary edema, pulmonary embolus, bacterial pneumonia, respiratory failure, renal failure and stroke.

Anesthesia is always a risk, but significantly so for the elderly. Currently patients are spending less time in the hospital following surgical intervention making our responsibility for recognition acute. Certain surgical procedures also contribute to an increase risk for delirium. The most significant rates for the development of delirium occur following a hip fracture. Post-operative delirium is associated with intraoperative blood loss, increased postoperative blood transfusions, and postoperative hematocrit levels less than 30%.

All physicians and nurses are responsible for continuing their education to ensure optimal patient care. Even when continuing education is not mandated, it remains an ethical responsibility. Incorporation of reliable tools to assess mental status on a routine basis would aid in the early recognition of a potentially reversible life-threatening condition know as delirium.

CHAPTER   1 7

Delirium in the Nursing Home

It has been said many times that America is growing old. Since 1996, one American turns fifty years of age every seven seconds, and will continue to do so for the next sixteen years. In addition, the life expectancy of Americans increases significantly with each generation. The incidence of older persons experiencing mental health problems is relatively small, only 20% of people over fifty-five years of age are diagnosed with a psychiatric illness. The most common problems include anxiety, depression and dementia. Delirium is mentioned as commonly occurring but it is not documented due to its lack of recognition. The numbers of individuals experiencing delirium in the nursing home are as follows:

10–40% of all elderly upon admission to hospital

25–60% following admission

Affects 2.3 million hospitalized elderly

Estimated cost is $4 billion per year

The amount of money that unrecognized delirium costs the United States is difficult to assess. What is known is the costly complications of untreated cases.

Risk Factors Present*	Risk of Delirium	Risk of Death or Nursing Home Placement
0 = Low risk	3%	3%
1 or 2 = Intermediate risk	16%	14%
3 or 4 + High risk	32%	26%

Predisposing factors

- Neurotransmitter dysfunction, neuronal loss
- Homeostatic and immune mechanisms are less efficient
- Decreased ability to metabolize medications
- Changes in vision and hearing
- Cardiovascular changes—decline in cardiac output

The human and economic consequences of delirium are devastating. The elderly are more likely to encounter longer hospitalizations, placement in extended-care facilities and higher healthcare cost as a result of the lack of recognition and treatment of delirium (Naylor, 2003).

Educating staff to recognize the difference between confusion caused by delirium and/or dementia is crucial. This differentiation is complicated by the fact that persons with a diagnosis of dementia are at the greatest risk of developing delirium (Schofield, 2002). Remembering that the cognitive changes that occur with dementia are progressively slow and the changes occurring with delirium are sudden will assist in the recognition and treatment of delirium.

---

*Risk factors: vision impairment, severe illness, cognitive impairment, and high blood urea nitrogen-creatinine ratio. Adapted from Inouye, S. K., et al. *Ann Internal Medicine* 1993.

In 1987, under the Omnibus Budget Reconciliation Act, the Minimum Data Set (MDS) was brought to the nursing home for use in assessing the needs of the elderly patient (Culp, Mentes, & McConnell 2001). As part of the MDS the Resident Assessment Instrument was introduced, which includes indicators for delirium. A comparison of the MDS 1 and MDS 2 criteria are listed below.

The criterion below offers the healthcare provider the information necessary to recognize delirium and initiate interventions appropriate for the condition.

Comparison of the MDS 1.0 & MDS 2.0; Delirium Indicators

MDS 1.0	**MDS 2.0**
Less alert, easily distracted	Easily distracted
Changing awareness of environment	Periods of altered perception or awareness of surroundings
Episodes of incoherent speech	Episodes of disorganized speech
Periods of motor restlessness or lethargy	Periods of restlessness Periods of lethargy
None of the above	Mental function varies over the course of the day
Score 0 absent or 1 present during the past 7 days	Score 0 absent, 1 present no of recent onset, or 2 present during past 7 days appears different from resident's usual behavior

These standards are utilized for rationalizing the care required for each resident. Typically one nurse is hired and her job is dedicated to reviewing the medical records of residents and documenting the data collected. The information gathered goes no farther than the sheets it is assembled upon.

Amassing data specifically for the purpose of meeting a requirement is useless. There is no communication loop established to bring the information back to the care providers. The information contained in the MDS is invaluable for the ongoing individualized care provided for each resident. If a feedback loop were established that would bring the current information back to nurses responsible for providing care, changes in cognitive and functional status would potentially reflect potential physiological causes, and interventions aimed at treating this cause could be eliminated. Elimination of the underlying cause would improve resident outcomes.

Delirium at the End of Life

M inimal literature is available discussing delirium in the individual with a terminal illness. Information is scarce concerning the frequency, clinical course, and timing of delirium in patients with cancer. Even less is published concerning delirium related to other terminal illnesses. Death happens as it may. No one can predict its arrival. With terminal illness people can experience several crises that threaten their life. The first priority of health care practitioners is to know the dying individuals wishes. These desires must be honored above all others. Having established the, the condition of delirium can be handled appropriately.

Dying causes drastic physiological changes within the body. Waste products are produced and the body is no longer able to eliminate them effectively. The body's ability to maintain a state of equilibrium has been challenged. A complication caused by these changes is a state of delirium in the dying patient. The clinical picture resembles other manifestations described earlier. Common characteristics include disturbances in arousal, awareness of surroundings, perception, cognition and psychomotor activities. Symptoms tend to increase in severity during the nighttime hours. It has been suggested that the physiological changes that occur near death are a protective mechanism. These changes offer the patient relief from the suffering immediately prior to death.

As stated earlier, delirium constitutes a medical emergency. How healthcare practitioners respond to delirium in the terminally ill client depends on the condition of the client and the stated wishes of the client. If the cause of the delirious state pertains to an area where the person has stated they desire intervention, health care practitioners must intervene accordingly. If the individual has expressed there be no intervention, palliative measures may be continued. Identifying the cause of delirium in the dying client must be a priority. Actions in response to the cause depend on each individual situation. Delirium in the terminally client can alter quality of life for the patient and the family.

Decisions regarding treatment must be based on the expressed wishes of the dying patient. Prior to the stage of active dying, delirium can negatively impact the person's involvement in life. Treatment for delirium during these times allows the patient to maintain activities that they choose to be a part of. Treatment also decreases the possibility of complications that increase the risk of complications. In turn, these complications negatively impact the person's general physical condition.

The stage of active dying can produce alterations in mental status. Altered mental status with restlessness can be difficult for the family to observe. Understanding that the client is experiencing a normal response to the dying process provides the loved ones with comfort in knowing the patient is not in distress.

As stated many times earlier, delirium is a medical emergency. This is true except in the case of the individual who is dying. As the body prepares for the death event, numerous body systems are failing and the patient becomes delirious. Conditions such as vital organ failure, analgesic toxicity, electrolyte imbalances, inadequate oxygenation of vital organs, dehydration and sepsis are the most common reasons underlying the presence of delirium in the terminally ill patient (Wakefield & Johnson, 2001).

CHAPTER 19

Complications

Individuals who demonstrate delirium are at risk for several complications. Safety risks include falls leading to broken bones, tissue injury and lacerations. Inactivity leads to pneumonia, pressure sores, urinary tract infections, edema, blood clots, and joint contractures. Confusion leads to malnutrition, dehydration internal distress, agitation, mistrust of loved ones and healthcare providers and refusal to follow recommended medical treatments. Death is the most serious complication and is common when delirium is undetected and not treated. If associated medical conditions are not treated, individuals may also die.

Fick and Foreman (2000) conducted a study on the consequences of not recognizing delirium. Twelve patients were found to be incontinent of urine even though they had been observed asking to use the bathroom. Sixty-seven percent experienced significant weight loss. One participant lost more than ten pounds in three weeks prior to hospitalization. Her family made attempts to feed her but she refused. She was admitted to the hospital for eight days, discharged and re-admitted for another seven days. Her family complained that when they fed her she would fall asleep with food in her mouth. Her second admission led to placement in a nursing home where she fell and broke her hip. She was once again admitted to the hospital for a ten-day stay. Again she was weighed and had lost seventeen pounds during this four-week course. Weight loss of such significance severely compromises a person's ability to actively participate in their life. Even the most mundane task requires a level of energy that is no longer available. This vulnerable state also predisposes a person to infection.

In a weakened state, the body is a welcoming respite for opportunistic agents. These agents can infect the kidneys, lungs, mouth, integumentary lesions or systemically. Once these agents enter the body, with its defenses already compromised, the invading agent has free reign. This added insult limits a person's ability to be independent.

Dependency brings with it a variety of issues. Pressure sores, blood clots, atelectasis, and joint contractures. Once the skin is broken, the width and depth of a decubiti spread initiating a cascade of physical decline. Decubiti are painful and require intense treatment regimes. Healing is slow and quality of life is negatively impacted. Blood clots are potentially lethal and treatment brings risks. Joint contractures are permanent and incapacitate a person making them dependent on others for care.

Outcomes:

- 2.3 million elderly affected yearly
- 17.5 additional inpatient days
- Increased in-hospital and post-discharge mortality
- Increased risk of institutional placement post-discharge
- Estimated cost $4 billion in annual excess health care dollars

CHAPTER 20

Conclusions

Failure to recognize delirium or misdiagnosing delirium has significant consequences. If delirium is not recognized in due time, the prognosis of the patient is poor. In addition, morbidity and mortality rates increase. This increase raises the financial strain on the healthcare system, in addition to prematurely raising the risk of out of home placement.

It is imperative that healthcare provides become educated to the clinical presentation of the client with delirium, attain knowledge of the predisposing factors that lead to delirium and intervene expediently to alleviate complications.

Maintaining personal/professional education is not the only responsibility of the healthcare practitioner. It is important to educate patients and their loved ones on the signs/symptoms of delirium. Advanced explanation allows the patient to make decisions about interventions they desire if delirium exhibits itself. Education also empowers loved ones to feel a sense of comfort knowing that the behavior of the individual is based on an underlying cause and not necessarily dementia or another tragic condition. It further allows loved ones the ability for decision-making regarding future treatment and care following discharge from an institution. This education has the potential for earlier recognition of delirium, potentially resulting in earlier treatment. This, in turn will lower the morbidity and mortality rates and ease the financial strain that this condition produces.

GLOSSARY

Acetylcholine	A chemical of the cholinergic neurotransmitting system. It is responsible for the transfer of nerve impulses across the synapses.
Addiction	Inability to abstain from drug use, accompanied by drug intolerance and withdrawal.
Adverse reaction	A harmful, unintended reaction to a drug administered in a normal dose.
Affect	A subjectively experienced feeling state or emotion that is expressed by observable behavior.
Agnosia	Lack of sensory-perceptual ability to recognize objects.
Akathisia	Subjective sense of restlessness with a perceived need to pace or move continuously.
Anhedonia	Persistently depressed mood and loss of interest or pleasure in almost all activities. Inability to find joy in daily activities.

Anticholinergic	A group of drugs that reduce spasms of certain smooth muscles, decrease gastric, bronchial and salivary secretions through the blocking of vagal impulses.
Anticholinesterase	A "check and balance" enzyme responsible for regulating and lowering levels of acetylcholine and preventing overproduction.
Antihistamines	Chemicals, synthetics, and natural herbs, that possess anti-allergic properties. They reduce the proliferation of histamine H1-responsible for allergic symptoms.
Antioxidants	Chemical found in fruits, vegetables, and herbs that prevent damage from free radicals and chemical oxidation.
Antipsychotics	A substance that counteracts or diminishes symptoms of psychosis.
Anxiety	State where a person has strong feelings or worry or dread, where source is non-specific or unknown.
Anxiolytics	Synthetic chemicals and herbs that reduce anxiety.
Aphasia	Difficulty or inability to recall words.
Apraxia	An impairment in the ability to manipulate objects or perform purposeful acts.
Ataxia	An inability to coordinate movement, which results in abnormal gait and staggering.
Atrophy	Shrinkage of tissues.
Cholinergic	Relates to the parasympathetic nervous system that utilizes acetylcholine as a neurotransmitter.

Cholinergic Nerve Receptor	Type of nerve receptor of the parasympathetic nervous system. Located at the synapse, it involves the release and reuptake of the neurotransmitter acetylcholine.
Cognition	The mental process characterized by knowing, thinking, learning and judging.
Concentration	The effortful, deliberate and heightened state of attention in which irrelevant stimuli are deliberately excluded from conscious awareness.
Confusion	A mental state in which reaction to environmental stimuli are inappropriate; person is bewildered and unable to orient self.
Delirium	An acute change in a person's level of cognition and consciousness that occurs over a short period of time.
Delusion	Mental disorder leading to false and unshakable beliefs
Denial	An unconscious defense mechanism to protect against realities that the individual is not able to cope with.
Depression	An on-going sadness that may stand alone or accompany anxiety or dementia. Can be caused by other physical disease entities and/or medications.
DSM-IV TR	Diagnostic and Statistical manual, 4th edition Text Revision. Classification for mental disorders.
Dysarthia	Problems with articulation.
Dysnomia	Impaired sense of smell.
Dysgraphia	Difficulty writing.

Extrapyramidal Symptoms	A Parkinson-like syndrome involving drooling, involuntary hand movements and an inability to remain still.
Hallucinations	A sensory disturbance involving vision and hearing causing an individual to hear or see things that do not exist.
Herbal	Naturally occurring plant substances such as flowers, bark, or roots that are used to treat most known diseases and illnesses.
Hyperkinesia	Abnormally reactive motor responses.
Hypokinesia	Abnormally diminished motor activity.
Illusion	Misinterpretation of a real experience.
Iatrogenic	An unfavorable response to therapy induced by the therapeutic effort itself.
Insight	The ability of a person to observe himself and his situation and to interpret this observation in a way that is consistent with the perceptions of others.
Judgment	The ability to recognize social situations and the socially appropriate or safe response to such situation and to apply the correct response when faced with the real situation.
Memory	The intellectual function that registers stimuli, stores them around past perceptions and retrieves then at will.
Mood	A pervasive and sustained emotion that may markedly color a person's perception of the world.
Neuroleptic	A substance that alters consciousness, creating indifference to surroundings and reducing motor activity.

Neuroleptic Malignant Syndrome
A disorder associated with sudden fever, rigidity, tachycardia, hypertension, and decreased levels of consciousness.

Neurotransmitter
A combination of brain chemicals (amino acids) that transmit nerve impulses across synapses. There are over 50 neurotransmitters in the brain.

Paranoid
Neurotic or psychotic false ideations that people are plotting against them, talking about them, or are intent on doing them harm.

Perception
The intellectual function that integrates sensory impression into meaningful data and to memory. Perceptual functions include such activities as awareness, recognition, discrimination, patterning, and orientation.

Perseveration
The constant repetition of an apparently meaningless word or phrase.

Pharmacodynamics
The study of the mechanism of action of a drug and the biochemical and physiologic effect.

Pharmacokinetics
Absorption, distribution, metabolism, and excretion of a drug in the body.

Premorbid
Proceeding the occurrence of disease.

Proprioception
Sensations from within the body regarding spatial position and muscular activity.

Status Epilepticus
A condition in which one major attack of epilepsy succeeds another with little or no intermission.

REFERENCES

Brown, T. M. & Boyle, M. F. (2002). Delirium. *Behavioral Management Journal;* vol. 325(21), 644–647.

Burgener Sandy C, Dickerson-Putman Jeannette. (1999). Assessing patients in the early stages of irreversible dementia; the relevance of patient perspective. *Journal of Gerontological Nursing,* February, 33–41.

Cobb, J,. Glantz, M., Martin, E., Paul-Simon, A., Cole, B., & Corless, I. (2000). Delirium in patients with cancer at the end of life. *Cancer Practice*, vol. 8(4) 172–177.

Culp, K, Mentes, J, & McConnell, E. (2001).Studying acute confusion in long-term care: Clinical investigation or secondary data analysis using the minimum data set? *Journal of Gerontological Nursing*, vol. 27(4) 41–48.

Fick, D. & Foreman, M. (2000). Consequences of not recognizing delirium superimposed on dementia in hospitalized elderly individuals. *Journal of Gerontological Nursing*, vol. 26(1), 30–40.

Flacker, J., Marcantonio, E. (1998). Delirium in the elderly. *Aging*, 13(2), 119–130.

Foreman, M., Wakefield, B., Culp, K., & Milisen, K. (2001). Delirium in elderly patients: An overview of the state of the science. *Journal of Gerontological Nursing*, vol. 27(4) 12–20.

Inouye, S. K., van Dyck, C. H., Alessi, C. A., Balkin, S., Siegal, A. P., & Horwitz, R.I. (1990). Clarifying confusion: The confusion assessment method. A new method for detection of delirium. *Annuals of Internal Medicine*, 113(12), 941–948.

Inouye, S. K., Viscoli, C. M., Horwitz, R. I. et al. (1993). A predictive model for delirium in hospitalized elderly medical patients based on admission characteristics. *Annuals of Internal Medicine*, 119: 474–481.

Inouye, S. K. (2002). Foreword. In J. Lindesay, K. Rockwood, & A. Macdonald, (Eds.), *Delirium in Old Age* (pp. v–vi). Oxford: Oxford Press.

Insel, K. C., & Badger, T. A. (2002). Deciphering the 4 D's: cognitive decline, delirium, depression and dementia—a review. *Journal of Advanced Nursing*, vol. 38(4), 360–368.

Justice, Marcia. (2000). Does "ICU psychosis" really exist? *Critical Care Nurse*, 20(3), 28–39.

Hayes, K. S. (2000). Challenges in emergency care: The geriatric patient. *Journal of Emergency Nursing*, 26:430–435.

Henry, M. (2002). Descending into delirium. *American Journal of Nursing*, vol. 102(3), 49–55.

Laplante, J, & Cole, M. (2001). Detection of delirium using the Confusion Assessment Method. *Journal of Gerontological Nursing*, vol. 27(2), 16–23.

Meagher, D. (2001). Delirium: optimizing management. *Behavioral Management Journal*, vol. 332(20) 144–149.

McElhaney, J. (2002). Delirium in elderly patients: How you can help. *Consultant*, 42(4), 488–490.

Naylor, M. (2003). Delirium, Depression Often Overlooked. *American Journal of Nursing*, vol. 103(5), 116.

O'Brien, D. (2002). Acute postoperative delirium: Definitions, incidence, recognition, and interventions. *Journal of Perianesthesia Nursing,* vol.17 (6), 384–392.

Rabinowitz, T. (2002). Delirium: An important (but often unrecognized) clinical syndrome. *Current Psychiatry Report,* 4(3), 202–208.

Ranjan, A. (2001). Recognizing delirium in the hospitalized elderly. *Family Practice Recertification,* vol. 23(7), 11–18.

Rapp, C. G., (2001). Acute confusion/delirium protocol. *Journal of Gerontological Nursing,* vol. 27(4), 21–33.

Richardson, S. (2003). Delirium: Assessment and treatment of the elderly patient. *The American Journal for Nurse Practitioners,* vol. 7(1). 9–15.

Roberts, B. L. (2001). Managing delirium in adult intensive care patients. *Critical Care Nurse,* 21(1), 48–55.

Rockwood, K., Lindesay, J. (2002). The concept of Delirium: Historical antecedents and present meaning. In J. Lindesay, K. Rockwood, & A. Macdonald, (Eds.), *Delirium in Old Age* (pp.1–8). Oxford: Oxford Press.

Sammuels, S., Evers, M. (2002). Delirium: Pragmatic guidance for managing a common confounding and sometimes lethal condition. *Geriatrics,* 57(6),33–40.

Sanders, A. B. (2002). Missed delirium in older emergency department patients: A quality-of-care problem. *Annals of Emergency Medicine,* 39:338–341.

Schofield, I. (2002). Assessing for delirium. *Nursing Older People,* vol. 14(7), 31–33.

Schofield, I. & Dewing, J. (2001). The nursing contribution to the care of older people with a delirium in acute care settings. *Nursing Older People,* 13(1), 21–35.

Schuurmans, M., Duursma, S., & Shortridge-Baggett, L. (2001). Early recognition of delirium: Review of the literature. *Journal of Clinical Nursing*, 10:721–729.

Stein-Parbury, J. & McKinley, S. (2000). Patients' experience of being in an intensive care unit: a select literature review. *American Journal of Critical Care*, 9(1), 20–27.

Truman, B, & Wesley, E. (2003). Using the Confusion Assessment Method for the intensive care unit. *Critical Care Nurse*, 23(2),25–38.

Trzepacz, P., van der Mast, R. (2002). The neuropathophysiology of delirium. In J. Lindesay, K. Rockwood, & A. Macdonald, (Eds.), *Delirium in Old Age* (pp.51–90). Oxford: Oxford Press.

Wakefield, B & Johnson, J. (2001). Acute confusion in terminally hospitalized patients. *Journal of Gerontological Nursing*, vol. 27(4), 49–55.

Weindel, I. (2002). A case study of postoperative delirium. *AORN Journal*, vol. 75(3), 595–599.

Wright, S. (2000). Delirium in the elderly. *Advance for Nurse Practitioners*, vol. 8(4), 71–74.

http://www.1uphealth.com

http://www.psych.org

http://www.merk.com/pubs/mm_geriatrics/sec5/ch39.htm

THE CONFUSION ASSESSMENT
METHOD (CAM)*

Feature 1: ACUTE ONSET AND FLUCTUATING COURSE

This feature is obtained from a family member or nurse and is shown by positive responses to the following questions:

- Is there evidence of an acute change in mental status from the patient's baseline?
- Did the (abnormal) behavior fluctuate during the day—that is, tend to come and go, or increase and decrease in severity?

Feature 2: INATTENTION

This feature is shown by a positive response to the following question:

- Did the patient have difficulty focusing attention—for example, being easily distractible, or having difficulty keeping track of what was being said?

Feature 3: DISORGANIZED THINKING

This feature is shown by a positive response to the following question:

- Was the patient's thinking disorganized or incoherent, such as rambling or irrelevant conversation, unclear or illogical flow of ideas, or unpredictable switching from subject to subject?

Feature 4: ALTERED LEVEL OF CONSCIOUSNESS

This feature is shown if any other than "alert" is given to the following question:

- Overall how would you rate this patient's level of consciousness? Alert (normal), vigilant (hyper alert), lethargic (drowsy, easily aroused), stupor (difficult to arouse), or coma (unrousable)?

THE DIAGNOSIS OF DELIRIUM BY CAM REQUIRES THE PRESENCE OF FEATURES 1 & 2 AND EITHER 3 OR 4

STUDY PACKAGE
CONTINUING EDUCATION
CREDIT INFORMATION

DELIRIUM
THE MISTAKEN CONFUSION

Thank you for choosing PESI Healthcare as your continuing education provider. Our goal is to provide you with current, accurate and practical information from the most experienced and knowledgeable speakers and authors.

Listed below are the continuing education credit(s) currently available for this self-study package. ***Please note, your state licensing board dictates whether self study is an acceptable form of continuing education. Please refer to your state rules and regulations.*

Counselors: PESI HealthCare, LLC is recognized by the National Board for Certified Counselors to offer continuing education for National Certified Counselors. Provider #: 5896. We adhere to NBCC Continuing Education Guidelines. These self-study materials qualify for 1.5 contact hours.

Psychologists: PESI is approved by the American Psychological Association to offer continuing education for psychologists. PESI maintains responsibility for the material. PESI is offering this self-study activity for 1.5 hours of continuing education credit.

Social Workers: PESI HealthCare, 1030, is approved as a provider for social work continuing education by the Association of Social Work Boards (ASWB), (540-829-6880) through the Approved Continuing Education (ACE) program. Licensed Social Workers should contact their individual state boards to determine self-study approval and to review continuing education requirements for licensure renewal. Social Workers will receive 1.5 continuing education clock hours for completing this self-study material.

Addiction Counselors: PESI HealthCare, LLC is a Provider approved by NAADAC Approved Education Provider Program. Provider #: 366. These self-study materials qualify for 1.8 contact hours.

Nurses: PESI HealthCare, LLC, Eau Claire is an approved provider of continuing nursing education by the Wisconsin Nurses Association Continuing Education Approval Program Committee, an accredited approver by the American Nurses Credentialing Center's Commission on Accreditation. This approval is accepted and/or recognized by all state nurses associations that adhere to the ANA criteria for accreditation. This learner directed educational activity qualifies for 1.8 contact hours. PESI Healthcare certification: CA #06538.

<u>Procedures</u>:   1. Read book.
                2. Complete the post-test/evaluation form and mail it along with payment to the address on the form.

Your completed test/evaluation will be graded. If you receive a passing score (80% and above), you will be mailed a certificate of successful completion with earned continuing education credits. If you do not pass the post-test, you will be sent a letter indicating areas of deficiency, references to the appropriate sections of the manual for review and your post-test. The post-test must be resubmitted and receive a passing grade before credit can be awarded.

If you have any questions, please feel free to contact our customer service department at 1-800-843-7763.

PESI HealthCare, LLC
200 SPRING ST. STE B, P.O. BOX 1000
EAU CLAIRE, WI 54702-1000

Product Number: ZHS008650   **CE Release Date:** 02/02/04

 **HealthCare**

P.O. Box 1000
Eau Claire, WI 54702
(800) 843-7763

Delirium
The Mistaken Confusion

ZNT008650

This home study package includes CONTINUING
EDUCATION FOR ONE PERSON: complete & return
this original post/test evaluation form.

ADDITIONAL PERSONS interested in receiving credit
may photocopy this form, complete and return with a
payment of $15.00 per person CE fee. A certificate of
successful completion will be mailed to you.

C.E. Fee: **$15**   Credit card # _____

Exp. Date _____

Signature _____

V-Code* _____ (***MC/VISA/Discover:** last 3-digit # on signature
panel on back of card.) (***American Express:** 4-digit # above account # on face
of card.)

**Mail to: PESI HealthCare, PO Box 1000, Eau Claire, WI 54702, or
Fax to: PESI HealthCare (800) 675-5026 (fax all pages)**

Name (please print): _____ _____ _____
                        LAST   FIRST   M.I.

Address: _____

City: _____ State: _____ Zip: _____

Daytime Phone: _____

Signature: _____

• Date you completed the PESI HC Tape/Manual Independent Package: _____

• Actual time (# of hours) taken to complete this offering: _____ hours

PROGRAM OBJECTIVES

How well did we do in achieving our seminar objectives?

	Excellent				Poor
Defining Delirium.	5	4	3	2	1
Identifying five clinical manifestations (symptoms) of delirium.	5	4	3	2	1
Listing three causes of delirium.	5	4	3	2	1
Identifying the most important initial step in treating delirium.	5	4	3	2	1
Recognizing the complications associated with unrecognized delirium.	5	4	3	2	1
Identifying the group of individuals at the greatest risk for the development of delirium.	5	4	3	2·	1
Listing three outcomes of unrecognized delirium.	5	4	3	2	1
Identifying the major components of non-pharmacological interventions when treating delirium.	5	4	3	2	1
Naming the clinical tool used most frequently and reliably in diagnosing delirium.	5	4	3	2	1

POST-TEST QUESTIONS (TRUE OR FALSE)

1. The definition of delirium includes a disturbance of consciousness.

   True or **False**

2. A general medical condition is a potential cause of delirium.

   True or **False**

3. Delirium and dementia have the same clinical presentation.

   True or **False**

4. Individuals who are delirious have altered sleep-wake cycles.

   True or **False**

5. The most important step in treating delirium is a calm environment.

   True or **False**

6. Congestive heart failure is a potential complication of delirium.

   True or **False**

7. Women who have just given birth are the group who are at the greatest risk for developing delirium.

   True or **False**

8. Unrecognized delirium increases long-term care placement.

   True or **False**

9. The MMSE is the most common tool used for diagnosing delirium

   True or **False**

10. Unrecognized delirium is responsible for $4billion in excess healthcare expense

    True or **False**

For additional forms and information on other PESI products, contact:
**Customer Service; PESI HEALTHCARE; P.O. Box 1000; Eau Claire, WI 54702
(Toll Free, 7 a.m.-5 p.m. central time, 800-843-7763).
www.pesihealthcare.com**

**Thank you for your comments.
We strive for excellence and we value your opinion.**

02/04